UNDER A TAIL-LIGHT MOON

DANIEL R. PHEN

Copyright © 2006 by Muse Eek Publishing Company
All Rights Reserved

ISBN 1-594899-28-2

No part of this publication may be reproduced, stored in a retrieval system, or transmitted, in any form or by any means, electronic, mechanical, photocopying, recording, or otherwise, without the prior written permission of the publisher

This publication can be purchased from your local bookstore or by contacting:
Muse Eek Publishing Company
P.O. Box 509
New York, NY 10276
USA
Phone: 212-473-7030
Fax: 212-473-4601
http://www.muse-eek.com
sales@muse-eek.com

Songs

6	WRONG
7	bad things
8	living death
9	the boy who removed his flesh
10	one square inch
11	one favor
12	heaven
13	Redemption
14	Shooting Star
15	widescreen
16	supine
17	Bending Sunlight
18	incandescence
19	hounds
20	Eclipse
21	hogs head
22	Napoleon
23	blue period
24	from where we came
25	Long the Way, Steep the Path
26	SOCIAL DADS
27	vampire
28	heat lightning
29	Home
30	Waltzing the Question
31	more than I
32	interior decoration
33	expectations of rain
34	Workspeak
35	Weight
36	Just Reward
37	spodiodi
38	haven

39	knife
40	someone to talk to
41	Shite
42	Pincushion
43	She
44	Necklace
45	underpants
46	living room dance
47	ship poetry
48	voyage home
49	*most likely 61 in 64*
50	gary
51	dead-ending
52	Socks
53	telemetry
54	tethered
55	Numb
56	Pheasants
57	*Kaptain Koin*
58	Girlsmoke
59	alien hand syndrome
60	pawn shop shopping
61	pawn shopping again
62	Dating Etiquette
63	desperation
64	Comfort
65	Needs
66	finale
67	because
68	
69	Pride of Las Vegas
70	purple valley
71	Xgirlfriend
72	run down the night
73	invitation
74	even the skies

The new
Olde Bags
are here

Handmade vintage style bags
at Hair Essence Salon
408 E. 8th st.
in Railroad Plaza.

Handmade vintage style bags
at Hair Essence Salon
408 E. 8th st.
in Railroad Plaza.

The new
Olde Bags
are here

The new
Olde Bags
are here

Handmade vintage style bags
at Hair Essence Salon
408 E. 8th st.
in Railroad Plaza.

Handmade vintage style bags
at Hair Essence Salon
408 E. 8th st.
in Railroad Plaza.

The new
Olde Bags
are here

WRONG

wrong runs alongside well-lit homes
thru darkened back yards
a susurrus of high wind
engulfing and washing the small house
buffets windows
shaking made beds and vacuumed rugs
rumples folded laundry
clinks the crystal
peeking in window
licked ice pressing the pane
searching for opening
to scream like an eagle
sight positioned by satellite
upon me where I sit
before this lonely
balanced meal

bad things

bad things are
bad things happen
always
locate you
safe at home
warm & comfy
snugged & sleepy
after lights are out
    you hear breaking glass
in another room
footsteps across the floor
    they stop in the kitchen
open the fridge
take a drink from your milk
finger your cutlery
think bad thoughts
danger abounds
bad things become
crazed catamounts
clawing their way
out of caved-in nightmares
    laying mad tracks
        for your face

living death

the category
was living death
i turned the channel
i held my breath
there was a spy
in the apartment
danger in the air
someone had glimpsed
derangement
submitted this line of inquiry
followed the path
of least refinement
to discover me
there
cowering in the corner
with a hammer
& railroad spike
chiseling
this epitaph shit
into the forehead
of bewilderment

the boy who removed his flesh

there's something
moving
under my skin
that can't get out
and can't stay in
eating nerve endings
sending warning
makes my skin jump
makes my skin twitch
erupt
in mild destruction
oozing,
crusting, suppurating,
feeding
off what it is hating
fatigue,
stress, nothingness.
yeah, Yahweh
reacheth out
laying fingerprint
upon my cheek
my offenses
too numerous
so heinous
as to make whys
    superfluous
shame & embarrassment
not only necessary
but long overdue
this burning mark
    his indictment.

one square inch

I cut
one square inch
of flesh
from my forearm
as an offering
to God.
the next week
one square inch
from my calf
and
the following week
peeled flesh from my stomach
all the while
praying
this wishbone of my body
might produce some one thing
of substance,
beauty, or quality,
except
this excruciating
pain of existence.

one favor

if
I don't grow old
I'll live
until I die
but
living fast
has grown me old
& I'm afraid
to be put away
where they stash
the invisible
away from youth's beauty
somewhere nowhere
in a cloud
of medication
beyond healing
beyond caring
    when I've always
cared for myself
    I implore you
those who institutionalize me
to take the time
waste a dime
drop one in my brainpan
for the sandman in me

I'm sorry
to fuck up your karma
but thank you
for the out

heaven

when i get to heaven
get my sitdown w/ jesus
learn the reasons
for all of the miseries
follow the travelogue
that was my life
acts of heroism
& indiscretions
get my welcome
into the gardens of paradise
take my cleansed soul
upon the golden byways
to say my howdies
to family & friends
wink at a few lovelies
lie down w/ lamb & lion
sleep dreamless
awaken to gabriel's trumpet solo
for breakfast
of fruit & fish
bread & wine

i'ma turn to god
raise up my goblet
in a toast
& say thank you for this
i love you
let's get on w/
another beautiful day

Redemption

sometimes
it is best
not to consider
things that must be done
but to lower your head
and move into it
determination cold on
bringing all force to bear
without mercy
or thought of recourse
    when the king returns
parasails down amongst us
all forecasts of redemption
and hopes for peace
will be
smashed to glory

eternity is everlasting

Shooting Star

desire rode a shooting star
dragging anchors of stakes & chains
under electric skyblue light
thudding & clanking
like sword or mace against shield
echoes ricochet heartwall
frigid unlit furnace
stored in barren basement
tortured by percussion
leaking faucet drip drop
squeeking stairstep threat
child in closet
whimpers
abandoned & alone
forgotten & afraid
quit like old dreams
fading like wallpaper
yesteryear's linoleum
hope's death.
fate dusts my lizardskin
leather weathered hide
daily
with funeral givings
& cemetery leavings
I've denied the broken hacksaw blade
moved to the farthest interior
to await & accept

widescreen

She was panoramic
as some big girls can seem
pretty as a widescreen picture
siren of the screen
confidant and careful
she had the world
by the balls
always bold
men's hearts she stole
young beautiful
she knew it all
only had
to make the call
blonde haired
but
she knew the number

supine

she lay supine
upon my loveseat
while i swigged
myself into the mood
she waited patiently
knowing me to be adroit
when aroused
smiled her crooked smile
of small amusement
    men
are such simple assholes
barely civil
still
 a friendly berth
in the harbour of night

Bending Sunlight

I'm bending sunlight
into jewelry
for you my love
I'm weaving sunlight
thru your hair
brushing it onto your cheeks
golden as your heart
precious
as all things tenuous and tender
these feelings promised
coloring life
astonishing
illuminating
glorifying
nourishing
warming
dancing radiantly
on
charms for your ears
rings for your toes

incandescence

I lick your skin
I taste your sin
I drink your sweat
your sour regret
comely in openness
I sense your essence
find the locus
of your turbulence
follow you
down warm sunfreckled meadows
to where flowing waters begin
where the blossom opens
to there inquire
upon ordinary become extraordinary
I eat you
repeat you
know you
like a hiking trail
this fern
that mound
    this
is where the swirlaround
    brush cloudscape from eyes

hounds

she had trained greyhounds
to run me down
    i killed some
she trained them to bite & chew
    i killed a few
i was slowed
i was wary
she trained them
to corner & bark
to wait for reinforcements
    i
    learned to kill from a distance
she resorted
to bigger dogs
the greyhounds
had served their purpose
inflicted their damage
made me fair game
either
i find land w/ close tree growth,
learn to move above ground
or die

Eclipse

Elizabeth
wanted to know
how it would feel
to put belladonna drops
into her eyes
to drink absinthe
to smoke opium
sip laudenaum
to kill a man
with a hat pin
while held in his embrace
kissing
beneath a gas lamp
during a lunar eclipse
& I
love
the wonder in her.

hog's head

my madam
she's bought a hog's head
to boil w/ the beans
cabbage and onion greens
sage, bayleaf, garlic, and pepper
rice and red wine
and more for our cups
a little nippa to go w/ our supper
as the stewpot bubbles
above steams the puddin
vanilla, brown sugare, butter, & eggs
whipped w/ a loaf a day old
bread to give it legs
whipped like the cream & sugare
sittin in a bowl of cold water
whilst i sit
 feet up before the fire
lighting this pipefull
admiring our cook
the squire's daughter

Napoleon

i stand on edge
of the porch
on the edge
of civilization
and unleash a stream
of steaming morning piss
into my lady's flowerbed
where she kneels
digs, weeds, and waters

i hold my edge
in my calloused hand
whistling
into morning humidity
mixing fragrance and colour
for lady to pluck
and place as centerpiece
upon Napoleon's dining table

blue period

the piano
is perfect mathematics
linear
laid like love outstretched
a touch instrument
able to dampen to a whisper
or thunder percussively
forever
one floor away
beyond doors and below
Van Gogh's basement
got some
shit goin' down
weird scenes
artistic dispute
welded, painted & posed
art savant
standing alone in darkness
creating
sunshine on the river
w/ a galvanized appearance
gold, silver, gray fishscale ripples
waving in sequence
shimmering brass tassels
flickering
fracturing images
communicating w/ linelength
color strength
illumination
reflective obsidian mirrors
yearning
deeper blue depression
lowering the basement floor
opening the dikes

from where we came

this is from where we came
the sound of our hearts
pounding softly in sneakers
while we lay recumbent in womb
gently wave rocking
which we alter
with the motion
of our limbs
establishing sensations
of rhythm
drum turnarounds
repeated in ripples
percussive injections
reflective umbilical nimbus
rocking softly
absorbing
mama talk
papa song
oldsters mumble chuckling
baby hears these things
and kicks
tiny stomps
romp through his musical roots
    it's his voice
instinctive beginning
communication
we splash, tic, & thunder
as music
from where we came

Long the Way, Steep the Path

    i want it good
    for the kids
    don't you?
    the moon, stars
    clear blue sea
    rainfall on green grasses
    electric cars
    wind energy
    organic vegetables
    range raised chicken
    safety for whales & manatee
    conglomerates that care
    love
    that stands the test of time
    hope
    respect
    equality
    role models with a little class
    morals
    ethics
    future
    a family
        I want it good for the kids,
        don't you?
            I guess we all do.

SOCIAL DADS

sometimes my family
would hang-out w/ other families,
someone dad worked w/
or had gone to school w/ or something.
they would send us kids outside to play
so they could do those
adult things,
drink, flirt, joke & lie.
we kids would do our part
fight, flirt, scream, lie,
run wild until night closed us down.
during the skirmish
some strange kid would point through the window
and say to me,
your dad seems pretty neat
& i would agree
knowing that the man in the window
was not my dad
that was a guy never home at our house.
the real guy
from our house
was scarey & selfish,
the farthest thing from neat.

we would all look at each other silently
wondering about the monster we knew.
why he lived at our house.
why we couldn't take our chances elsewhere,
in the woods or alleys.
as if something out there might be worse yet,
but,
we dare not speak.
our eyes our only language
scared even among siblings
lest the dadthing overhear
or read our minds

vampire

one sister
turned to the others & said
i think dad's a vampire
cuz he only sleeps
during movies
i woke up at three
he was doin laundry
i got up at five
after a bad dream
that he wasn't alive
he was in the kitchen
drinking coffee
staring out the window
he's been doin that lately
guess he's lonely
growing darker
quieter
becoming a different guy
sometimes i can see through him
like he's not really there
but
when we get up in the morning
breakfast is always hot & ready
& dad's grinning that he loves us

heat lightning

it's just heat lightning, honey
no rain gonna cool us tonight
no breeze stir, no wind blow
ain't gwine be tornado
just the sweating
sweltering
lay on top of the sheets
turn the pillow over
fan on high
dry out the sinuses
feel like you wanna die
sleeplessness

Home

Outside
hellflame hound snarls
teeth bared
scaring away stars
as they converse
about future
until it becomes obsolete
inside i hide
replete in talking smart house
sound on sound surround
speaking security system
viewed on HD Plasma TV
vignette of mechanism
sings new eroticism
a composition
made up of sales phrases
running a shortloop
synthetic download
to the comfort of robotic vacuum color

Waltzing the Question

She
wanted to talk it out
had her arguments
all lined up
like
shotglasses on a college bar
knowing
but pretending she didn't
that
men would rather walk
than talk
would rather say goodbye
or die
than
waltz the same sorry question
around the tabletop
one more time

more than I

more than i could ever stand
to lose
was what led me
past your bed
as you dreamed
of someone younger
my footsteps
whispering
delicately
to your desires
as your
swollen nipples
bend the silk sheets

i notice
and stop
    stoop to kiss your forehead
which
in your unconsciousness
becomes something quite else

interior decoration

she said i bought you....
i knew what she meant
as she gestured around

that i was spent
ready to be disposed of
without worth
a trashthing
    she was dark and pale
assuredly company for genius
denizen of sophistication
nestled among her things antique
listening to my fading footsteps
falling fast in the fading firelight

i would transform her surroundings
magically once again
with my departure

expectations of rain

the rains returned this afternoon
weather seasoning
shortening days
a windy gray tutelage
ours
 was love
that was not love
could not alter or change
as love must
to survive hypothermia
vanquish the mists & madness
sorrow beyond pain's beating
pressed us in death's caress
shadows by lightning lit
made wall puppets of our emotion
showers storm w/ crashing thunder
we flamed out
 like spent matches

Workspeak

I come from work
where they speak
in
fuck this
& fuck that
I come from work
& fuck you
you pussy
you suck
everything you love
sucks
your every
belief
is piss running down your chickenshit leg
shit yourself & go home
you pile of puke
you piece of crap
your mommy pays me
to dance on my lap
    so
kiss my ass
suck my balls
lick my dick
you make me sick
fuckwad
I come from work
to a peaceful home
where I choose
to live alone.

Is it any wonder?

Weight

some of the kids at the plant
were giving me shit
like an AARP cat
shouldn't tear the sleeves
outta his t-shirt
   talking about my pipes
& cannons & shit
so
I walked past them
picked up the 150 lb
spool of cable
tensing every muscle
in my body
intestines screaming
 to climb out my asshole
walked back past them
& loaded it into the truck
stepping up
to the biggest boy
I looked him in the eyes
for a second
& said
J-man
I used to think
you were above this
 superiority bullshit
and fuck- all
glorification of youth & looks
but now I see
you're just another fat boy
with an ugly girlfriend

Just Reward

you struggle home
after a grueling days work
take a dump
pour yourself a drink
sit in your favorite chair
take a deep breath
exhale
& sip that just reward
as fine as anything
you've ever tasted
your first hit
takes your mind on a voyage
guiding you away from work thought
where you matter little
or not at all
cattle of the American workforce
the pounding constant dumbness
work, eat, work, sleep, work,
die
speech closes down
thought process ceases
every corridor & hallway
blocked
robbing the promise
from every personality trait
until finally
you become this
gray person
spewing this blood

spodiodi

i was taking
a late night walk
w/ a big ol' bottle of spodiodi
when assailed & surrounded
by buzzing
souped up vw beetles
four of them
containing 8 or 9 boys
asked if i wanted a ride
so i climb into the back of one
we continue cruising
no-one consults me
they lean out windows
to shout out at girls
i sit back, sunk down
observing w/ my spodiodi smile
as they start passing spliffs of lumbo
i am one w/ them
investigating the night
later they run low on gas
pull behind a lutheran church
get out a hose
take turns siphoning gas
from the church bus
5 or 6 gallons each
one kid puked on the stuff
then we all hop back in the bugs
buzz out into the night
i ask to get out after a bit
take a hit of my spodiodi
hoping not to have
pissed off
the augustana god

haven

they keeps askin for one thing
i tell them
it ain't that at all
but they insistent
usta what they know
parameters be fucked
where they from
they kings
what they want
thass what they gotta have
so i took them shoppin
lettum look over the goods
gave them some free taste

like all yall
i'm just workin to get my props
set aside some greenback dollar
take care o my peops
drive some zoom
but first
i gotta keep these fuckers happy
marketing like
get to that haven beyond boodle
yall know
what i's talking about

knife

he was a friend
of the knife
could not leave it
alone
put it down
solely by force of will
only to find
it back in his hand
again
rolling from side to side
in his palm
touching the ball of every finger
flicking open and closed
slipping smoothly from hand to hand
slitting the air
sharply,cleanly
silently
so deadly
keeping it company
in late solitude
interrupted only
by mumbled interjections
from a flickering tv

someone to talk to

I bring this girl
home from the bar
someone to talk to
while I drink & smoke
my way home to the tomb
back to the womb
pour us each a scotch
watch as she cuts herself a line
packs it up her nostrils
takes a drink of whiskey
doesn't even blink
guess she's frozen whatever needed it
she reaches for the joint
listening casually
Thelonious piano in stereo
I light a scented candle
cucumber
pull the big knife
from an end table drawer
lay the blade in the flame
slowly turning it
turning it black
lay it across the back
of my forearm
look into her green eyes
as the flesh bursts
something bubbles, smolders,
we watch time
go up in acrid smoke

Shite

threw the paint
upon the floor
I threw the bitch
against the wall
she threw the past
upon the fire
I said
her mouth
was big as her ass
she said my love
wasn't worth a bent dick
& my dick
was short as my memory
so I mentioned her sister
then her cousin Janelle
coming to get me
on a lightningbolt from hell
(I mean a 69 Chevelle)
she started throwing dishes
I reached for the keys

too late
for either of us
to speak the motherfucking
please.

the art
of desire
is not for the faint
of heart

Pincushion

you little prick,
she said
on a more personal note

I've never really liked you,
indeed,
in fact abhor you,
you make my liver ache

if I could isolate
each & everything
I hate about you
on the end of a long pin
you would
        fucking porcupine

She

She
leaves me
forget-me-nots
on my doorstep
I must see,
throw in the trash
immediately
before questions
are asked
for which answers
run naked
down moonlit alleys
giggling madly,
reciting in singsong,
who is she
what does she want
why are these flowers
tied in bouquets
bound in ivory ribbon

when will she stop?

is there an ending?

what did you do?

how could you?

Necklace

I was spokesman
for the diocese
lineman for the county
handyman fixerupper
and thought I'd heard
the entire story
when she spoke out
for what she believed in
confessed her innocence
whispered her aspiration
with bold honest confidence
      twas then that I noticed
      her coral necklace
      lay glowing
      in her cleavage
      like blood droplets
      sprinkled
      upon vanilla gold

underpants

You sent me
the perfume of you
on a pair
of underpants
by the US Mail
in a parchment wrap
in a cardboard box
warmed by sunlight
chilled by autumn evening
until reaching me
I reach into the parcel
lifting your present
& presence
to my face
inhaling your passion
painting memory
on this canvas
of closed eyelids
the living only you
sharply dark
in wispy folds
of pastel cloth.

living room dance

you
with your fear of romance
drop
your utilitarian panties
on my living room floor
and dance
like candlelight
upon the coffeetabletop
before me
as I
pour you another glass
of this
fine merlot
    the music
reaches crescendo
washing over us
as I take you
in my arms
your legs locking my waist
your butt
slamming into my happiness

ship poetry

in wordcrafting
paint sunset bloody
emptying heartbowl
upon fetid battleground
spirit silence flown
as death = life alone
the soul
life stole
sold down the lazy river
once again
bargained for
bent over barrel
alone as the sun
wanting only to warm you,
you, you
ten trillion light years away
the moon between us
the cliffs and canyon chasms
beyond climbing
fleet shadows filling valleys
to
plummet between dark mountains
firework screaming freefall stars
empty their light brightening
candleflame
fire upon the future

voyage home

upon mirror serenity of sea
slow therapy of whispered words
flutter winged indigo anxiety
relax and excite
spraypaint fervent feelings
in dark prison corners
ballpoint tattoo you
as the last little hope
white hot scorched lips
tremble for the
kissing
painfully humble hands
 offer out this carton of smokes
this chocolate bar
this pencil sketch
I am the soul of propriety
here to do your bidding
your bidness
your
nasty little thangs
hoping you don't
kick out the spark
leave me stranded
here in the dark

most likely 61 in 64

where were we
when dylan revisited hwy 61
north out of the cities
winding out his new 500
screaming his triumph
stopping for coffee & pie in duluth
staring out cafe windows
at the sweeping sheet of sapphire superior
& over the other shoulder
at broken cliffs of iron-range
before gassing up
donning dark shades
riding the twin lane blacktop
thru little & grand marais
hugging great lake curves
between towering trees
scattering gold & scarlet leaves
headed for ely
headwater of the mississippi
stopping at roadside turnaround
before the mapleleaf border
to decide
continue north
into the peace and solitude
or turn around
throw down the acoustic martin
pick up the telecaster
& face off against his loyal fans
hammering out a hot
tombstone blues

gary

i lost your dylan book
on the bus to deadwood
worried about it that night
hunted it down the next morning
i wasn't done reading it
and it wasn't mine
the surrounding hills spoke
to my sense of loss
accusing me of neglect
guilt made me circumspect
so i waited out a decent light
searched out the busdriver
and confessed my loss
    he said he'd found it
and another dark book
which i told him
was one i'd written
nothing to compare to the chronicles
but a spill of liquor
on the landscape of literature

dead ended

so many poems go nowhere
companion to the poet
who has nothing to say
spewing words with interesting sounds
that fall apart scurrying
after a story stranded
    dead-ended
ad infinitum
ad nauseam
syllables intoned intensively
imbuing import to sketch
a stretch to pay attention
I reawaken myself
force myself to read or listen
a lesson to learn
    how not to carve poetry.

Socks

I don't write for you
or anyone
don't care what you're interested in
or want to hear about

I only write
because of the aching void
    the need
to pull pain
like a tooth
thru taut tennis racket strings
and kick it
crying down the hall
out the window

to watch it
falling
into endless darkness
onto razor rocks

these words
turned inside out
like socks.

telemetry

you pull me
under
my Charybdis
as I wonder
about changing dynamics
of relationships

the telemetry
of you & I

where is line
of demarcation
avenue
between what you want
to receive
and what I
desire
to give you

tethered

we share
this very world
this every moment
under eternal star formations
winds sculpt borning landscapes
as us
two outlaws
run from like crimes
keep company in hiding
search place to bed down
quickstep escape dreams
before stifling waking screams
of more want
a constant scuffling
towards a paradise promise
from paranoid piranha princes
who predict knowledge of where it ends
    so
we're searching out alleyways
our souls
tattooed with disdain
tethered by a string
at arm's end.

Numb

surgical sawtooth
winter wind
slices thru jeans & anorak
cold cutting steel sleet
anesthetizes
presses pins thru flesh
steals lung capacity
glues lips to aching teeth
as feeling flees nose & ears
numbs dumb
fingers & feet
searing skin
blurring sight
tears freeze and forget to fall
winds intensify
moan & howl
showing snow which way to blow
driving it
and you before it.

Pheasants

So
the boss pheasant
struttin thru the corn stubble
looks over his pheasant troop
letting them see his lack of concern
he stops
spits in the dust and says
those fuckers
w/ their orange vests & shotguns
are almost on us
but
there's regular spacing
between them
so we gotta hit them gaps
fly like our asses are on fire
if we can get between them
before they know what's happenin
some of us high
some of us low
down the rows between them
    the fates be w/ us
they blow the shit outta each other
it's our only hope & chance
    let's go show them
whose damn cornfield this is
awright,
break on 5,

    5!

Kaptain Koin

a man came out of the laundrymat
to check on his daughter
see if she wanted a pop
or anything
she wanted to play outside
the weather was too nice to disagree
but he didn't see her
anywhere
and then when he did
it was in the passenger seat
of an SUV
at the corner
waiting on the light
he
got to the vehicle
just in time
to reach the driver through the window
before the light changed
choking everything to a standstill
his hands around the drivers throat
squeezing
as his daughter screamed
I'm ok Daddy
Daddy I'm ok I'm ok
long after cops showed up
to check on the stalled traffic
and even after they pulled their guns
he was still squeezing
squeezing

Girlsmoke

we were sitting
on top of the world
where clouds collide
in our young man's apartment
w/ girls
running beautiful
like wild horses
through our vigilant
afternoons & evenings
girlsmoke
the new dietfood
rose w/ their voices
mentholated
from the sidewalk
below my springsprung window
every puff
seasoned w/ dietcoke
their life elixir

alien hand syndrome

she had *alien hand syndrome*
and fought herself
in her sleep
    unaware
    involuntary
a neurological condition
always the left hand
    the evil sister
    always
    out of control
the consciousness
of alternate half
brains
warring
under
Martha Stewart
cotton sheets

pawn shop shopping

admiring artwork
my fingertips caress
the Gibson ES335
longingly
my girlfriend waits
patiently
tapping her toe
on the hardwood floor
the salesman approaches
once again
shaking his head
knowing I lack the cash
to purchase
wanting me
to break off this fateful
relationship
w/ elegant ebony lady
all curves symmetrical
lines & form perfect
I struggle to break free
from this dark magic
desire

pawn shopping again

the obvious
ducks into a doorway
tugging down the stocking
becoming a different entity
scribing an alternate destiny
slams open the entry
on immediate reality
douglas enters the pawn shop
turns & locks the door
vaults the low counter
rips the cellphone out the old man's hands
knocks the guy to the floor
dougie's dressed on the right
lowers his right hand
into his waistband
withdraws his chrome Eagle
there's a few things i need
& a few i just want, doug says,
kicking a steel toe boot into the owner's spine
i gotta lotta need
& i suspect
very little time
i want weapons
baby wants rocks
i'd take some laptops
old coins & watches
i can unload a little bling
start my own thing
so
don't you fucking move
cuz daddy's come shopping

Dating Etiquette

she started
laying her meds
upon the table surface
the stuff for moodswings
the bipolar & depression
panic & lethargy
telling me about the Docs
her twice a week sessions
the anger management
self esteem or lack thereof
varieties of abuse
vehemently dishing blame & excuse.
I told her,
hey, I got your back
you got any kinda amphetamine
there in your medicine sack
have I told you tonight
how your eyes catch the light
have you gotta place
we can raid the fridge?
maybe you gotta couch
I could use for awhile,
you seem like someone to trust
& I like your style
I'm a pretty nice guy
I'll do ya right
you're the queen of the world
I'll wear your colors
I'll be your knight
you need some help
and i'm ready to fight.
   you wanna
      be my girl?

desperation

I spotted her
asking around the bar
for some Dr Feelgood
offering up any of the 7 deadlies
when some slick weasel
w/ a rodeo buckle
scams her out into the lot
    curiosity
gets the best of me
convincing me to superhero
tangle in something
that shouldn't concern me
I think it was her gold nosering
and the illusion of innocence
I hoped would remain
throughout the evening
into some unknowable future
    so after the pedal-steel interlude
I broke my beer bottle
on the edge of the door
following into the dark car graveyard
trailing country music
and cigarette smoke.

Comfort

she laid her head
softly
upon my shoulder
said I love you
I'm so sorry
and
puked all over my shirt
as I stroked her back
telling her all was fine
while
my clothing steamed
in the evening chill
smelling
of something dead
and wine.

Needs

follow me to the bathroom
baby
I like
a girl with needs
a little belly
shows an appetite
a little hunger
feeds the wolf in me
i see
readiness
in your unsteadiness
my fingertips
touch your flannel cover
like an amputee arm
feels phantom hand-aches daily
even while curled into a fist.

finale

we wandered
hand in hand
down to the banks of the river
as premise
told her she might hear
explanation of my feelings
a growing estrangement
from life & her love
as of late
knowing
she considered it something
we could talk out,
    well,
conversation only prolongs
changing nada
so finally i turn to her
take her in my arms
& whisper
let's throw down here
in wet grass
& fuck this love goodbye

because

because i'm here waiting for you
everything i see is moving
every bird i see is flying
every girl i see is laughing
every flower i see is blooming
every voice i hear is singing
the wind is melody
the sun a blanket over me

because i'm waiting for you
everything i taste is honey
everything i say is funny
in all my pockets i find money
i cook things w/ exotic flavor
taste them & i know you'll savor
how i use dexterity
to favor you w/ quality

because i'm waiting for you
know not where you are
left me for favor
maybe forever
kidnapped, killed,
or gleefully kicking up your heels
lying beneath another
i slaughter my time
here
waiting for you
stagnate

she comes late
when all my inhibitions
are dying on the floor
gone, fled, MIA.
my monkey genes
kick in
i taste her in my mind
does she ever taste good
the exciting flavor
of danger and alcohol
wagonloads of spice
in a saucy apologetic smile

my fingers know the taste of you
are tempted by your elasticity
curving rise and fall of skin
gliding as waxed skis
on virgin slopes
always returning to the favorite
peaks and valleys
voracious in knowledge
navigating by excitement's breath
over here
and then a little to the left
my fingers
have known & loved you
forever
    don't desert me

leave me
at the mercy of another

Pride of Las Vegas

hey
did you hear
where that white tiger
took down that magician
out in Vegas?
fucking good work
I say,
other pipsqueak cocksucker
got away
I guess
would have
could have
made a jollier mess,
hopefully
them tigers
work thru their time off
to become more organized
and strategize.

purple valley

along your legs
between your knees
inside your thighs
are kisses
i have lost
drunkenly tossed
upon love's roiling waves
or waving curls
w/ the zeal
of a navy seal
toward a phalanx
of fulfillment fantasies
future hopes
fading slowly
as sunset
into some purple valley

Xgirlfriend

her walk was light & breezy
like a 60's pop song
i enjoyed wandering
her as a gallery
jaw-dropping colorburst
of light & shadow
bringing me stockstill
trying to tie together
these pieces of architecture
this dissapointing puzzle
where fractured timing
wasn't really the problem
i never
loved her more
than i do this very moment
when i sleepwalk
the red-eyed dawn
within this orbit
where once our ricochet
touched all walls
from when we did
promise & cherish
to now
we don't

run down the night

I was gonna run down the night
pull it's fucking panties down
check it's offerings
rip up a coupla galaxies
throw down a few monuments
howl out a symphony
frolic naked
through poppy fields

I was gonna run down the night
tattoo it's picture on my back
that contrast
of radiance
and all consuming black

invitation

i
invite the rain

walking
swimming
this chosen life
of stupidity,
and yet honor
my history
in refusing to change now
whether loneliness
solitude
or deathmask
face me down
i
remain loyal and true
arrow's path
cleaving the wind

even the skies

i lent my first book
to a lady from work
to read over the weekend,
when she returned it
she told me,
    you speak a darkness beyond black
    w/ a voice that kindles romance
    i hold time for you
    without pause
i
 looking at the wall
above her head
 replied
the line i've learned by heart
    i'm the death
    of all your mother's dreams
    when she imagines paradise
    in her daughter's happiness,

farewell,

this legion of misfortune
marches alone

THE AUTHOR

www.ingramcontent.com/pod-product-compliance
Lightning Source LLC
Chambersburg PA
CBHW031211090426
42736CB00009B/874